BUMPS,
POTHOLES &
OPPORTUNITIES

TRUE STORIES OF OVERCOMING LIFE'S TOUGHEST CHALLENGES

JON WRIGHT

innovo
PUBLISHING
innovopublishing.com

Published by Innovo Publishing, LLC
www.innovopublishing.com
1-888-546-2111

innovo
PUBLISHING
innovopublishing.com

Publishing quality books, eBooks, audiobooks, music, screenplays & courses for the Christian & wholesome markets since 2008.

BUMPS, POTHOLES & OPPORTUNITIES
True Stories of Overcoming Life's Toughest Challenges

Library of Congress Control Number: 2023917105
ISBN: 978-1-61314-959-1

Cover Design & Interior Layout: Innovo Publishing, LLC

Printed in the United States of America
U.S. Printing History
First Edition: 2023

Has God called you to create a Christ-centered or wholesome book, eBook, audiobook, music album, screenplay, or online course? Visit Innovo's educational center (cpportal.com) to learn how to accomplish your calling with excellence.

INTRODUCTION:
"LIFE AIN'T EASY"

When I was young, it seemed that life was easy. School wasn't that hard. Making friends was simple. Choices of work were plentiful, exciting, and profitable. Everyone that I knew was active, healthy, and happily moving forward in their journey.

I recall that when I had been married for a few years and our daughter was just a few months old, a "life coach" contacted me and tried to persuade me to enroll in his program. He asked questions like, "How is your marriage?" "Are you pleased with your job situation?" "Is your health where you would like it to be?" I wasn't trying to get rid of this guy or be rude, but I was happily married with a beautiful new baby girl. My job at the time was very challenging and very rewarding. I played sports, ran, lifted, and was very active. I was very satisfied with my health.

This poor guy kept asking me questions about every possible aspect of life, and I kept responding that all was good and that I wouldn't change a thing. Because it was the truth! After a while, he gave up on me.

A short time later, things started happening. Life became a little more difficult and didn't run as smoothly as in the past.

When you are driving down the road and hit a pothole, it can startle you. It can cause your heart to race and adrenaline to pulse through your body. It gets your attention. Hitting a bump of any kind can cause you to lose control and can put you in a ditch. Or you might not think that the bump was that big of a deal, only to discover later that you have blown a tire and are stuck in place and can't go any further. Experiencing a bump causes you to increase your focus and look for a clear path. Obviously, you try to avoid hitting bumps.

For the first time, I was experiencing real "bumps" in life.

Fortunately for me, I discovered that I wasn't jinxed or prone to bad luck. I learned that if we are fortunate to live long enough, we will all deal with some type of delay, challenge, or disappointment. We will experience a situation that gets our attention. Jaw-dropping news from the doctor. Family or work issues. The sickness or passing of a friend or family member. At some point, all of us will face a "bump."

Over the years, I have become acquainted with a lot of incredibly inspiring people who have faced some unique situations and weaved their way through them. Through their daily actions and reactions, these people have given me valuable lessons on everything from leadership, facing adversity, maximizing performance, patience, and finding the best in every situation. These friends are not celebrities. They are people that I've met through . . . well, just going through life.

A handful of these folks have graciously let me interview them and are willing to share their stories with the hope that their experiences will help someone else. I have specifically asked about their mindset in order to find out what helped them and what didn't help and to see if there are any common traits, tricks, or tactics.

I am a firm believer in not "reinventing the wheel" if possible. If someone has gone through a situation or solved a problem, then I will see if there is any common ground with their situation and mine and apply their experiences to lessen the challenge that I am facing. Imitation is the finest form of flattery, right? Learning from the actions they took, mistakes they made, and discoveries they found should make my path straighter and, hopefully, smoother.

The stories relayed in this little book might not exactly mirror your daily life, but the underlying lessons can be used in almost any situation. I hope that you find some encouragement from these words so that you feel better prepared to face life's *Bumps, Potholes & Opportunities.*

THOM

I first met Thom when my wife, daughter, and I moved back to the state of Georgia way back in the 1990s. He teaches and coaches at the same school as my wife. In addition to his academic responsibilities, Thom oversees and leads the boys' junior varsity and varsity soccer programs and has coached over a thousand soccer games throughout his career. His teams have won the state championship title six times and have played in the state championship game fourteen times.

Thom is good at what he does. He has been blessed with having kids in his program who happen to be very skilled in the sport of soccer, but it takes more than sheer talent and good genetics to build such an elite program. He encounters "bumps" as he prepares for each season and his teams compete.

When asked to describe the common traits of good players, he said,

> *All of my guys have been a cut above when I met them in seventh and eighth grade in terms of the way that they trained. It was their approach to how they practiced. Nobody worked harder.*

Confidence, not arrogance, is a key ingredient to performing well in any activity. The key to confidence is preparation.

> *The younger guys learn from the older guys how to practice and what is expected of them to keep the program moving forward. We don't have a handbook of a hundred rules to follow or anything, but we are going to do things the right way—how we act in the locker room, how we behave on the field, in the classroom, and on trips. We are not going to be noticed for the wrong reasons.*

Specific to his coaching philosophy, he said this:

> *I don't coach from criticism. I'm going to praise and encourage my players rather than beat them down. Focus on what they are doing right. I'm not a good yeller. My voice carries about four feet then hits the ground. [Smiles.] One year, I had two great players that were part of a team that ended up losing in the finals. You needed to put your foot through one guy to get his attention. The other guy was more sensitive. You wouldn't get anything out of him if you yelled at him. So, during this one game, the sensitive guy missed a wide-open potential go-ahead goal and needed to change his technique. He was flicking it instead of driving the ball. So I took him out to talk to him. When I subbed him, I could see his shoulders drop. Instead of making a scene and yelling at him, I whispered in his ear what he needs to do in that situation. Literally ten seconds after going back in the game, he had the exact same opportunity, and he scores doing just what I told him to do. He runs like sixty yards*

and jumps in my arms. He was mine forever. We keep in touch to this day. Now, if I would have buried him and yelled and benched him for a while, those things might not have happened.

All of Thom's teams have had different personalities, and it takes different methods and approaches to bring them together. He needs to be very direct with some. For others, it takes a more subtle messaging to get through to them. His approach will vary from year to year, depending on the makeup of his team. One year, he will address the areas for improvement in a group setting. The next year, he might find it more useful to speak to the players on an individual basis. It just depends.

I had this team one year . . . and they were good . . . [and they] couldn't take constructive criticism. They couldn't take it, especially in a public setting. They would wilt like flowers in the summer. So I would coach them one-on-one.

It's learning. It's learning the kids and taking the time to learn their personalities.

I had another group where we made the finals three out of four years. We were really, really, good. We never had a game in which we played poorly. Except one, where the game kept going back and forth. The other team would score a goal, and we would battle back to even it. We did some things that we usually didn't do late in the game and made some mistakes and lost. After the game, you could tell that our players were really upset and frustrated. We had a JV game the next day, and the kids that weren't playing in it gathered in our locker room. I set

11

up some chairs in front of the TV and sat in the back of the room. I had the remote and just hit "play." Didn't say a word. Never opened my mouth. Suddenly, they were saying things like, "I missed you there, sorry," and "we needed to be over here." We watched all the important points of the game, and they saw what needed to be corrected. When it was over, we were all walking out, and one player looked at me and said, "We will never lose again. We got it." And we won sixteen in a row and the state championship. It was just magical to watch it work.

Conducting a productive practice session and correcting mistakes is one thing, but mentally preparing a team to perform and succeed (whether it is in sports, business, or family) is another. *Getting up* for game time varies from one situation to another. Some sports, like football, are played in short bursts. Others, like soccer, are constant and require pacing. Football coaches will often manufacture *hype* to bring their team to an intense, emotionally high level. That doesn't work well in all situations.

Early in Thom's career, he was coaching in his first big game. If his team wins, then they go to the playoffs.

I put together this highlight video, and we watched it right before the game. We're going crazy and ready to go. We get on the field and find out that the other team is stuck in traffic. So we go back to the locker room. It was like being on a mountain and then going down to the valley. We were mentally and physically drained, and the game hadn't even started. We lost, and I don't even think that we scored a goal. I never did that again.

Now, he tries to avoid the peaks and valleys.

If the place has a gym, we'll go to it about an hour before the game starts and just relax. Some guys will shoot baskets, some will bounce a ball or whatever. We'll just turn on some music and relax. There's no hype. Soccer is a marathon and not a sprint. Adding emotion and tension to soccer guys is counterproductive.

Asked if he could provide any advice to soccer moms or dads, he responded,

Let your kids do a lot of stuff and try different things. If they want to concentrate on just one sport, they should be the ones telling you. It needs to be their decision; not yours. It's their game. Let them enjoy it. Sit back. Support the team, but don't yell your child's name. Your kid can hear you yelling their name, and so can the other kids. Don't undermine their effort. It's almost a form of abuse the way that some parents treat their kids during a practice or a game. Don't take the enjoyment away from the kid. You know, if you go to a kid's game in England— especially an academy game—parents can only clap. They will get kicked out if they open their mouth and start yelling at a player or a coach. There's a lot of wisdom in that.

I try to put together an environment where the player can flourish. It's their game. Let them have their "moment."

13

Thom was facing a different kind of competition when I first met him. Doctors had discovered a cancerous growth, which turned out to be a rare form of mesothelioma. Most patients with mesothelioma pass after a few years. It's not a great form of cancer, if there is such a thing. Fortunately, this form of the disease didn't attack the organs. It just grew, and the doctors were able to fully remove it.

> *My doctor said that this form of cancer has only happened twenty to twenty-five times in the last hundred years. It was a scary time, and it definitely changes how you see things— appreciating people, all of your opportunities and experiences, and all of the little things that happen in life.*

» **Coach/manage/parent from a position of praise and encouragement.**

» **Find the good and then build on it.**

» **Minimize the emotional ups and downs in a situation to maximize performance.**

» **We perform to the degree we prepare.**

TIM

The term *renaissance man* is defined as someone who has wide interests and is an expert in many areas. Tim's photo ought to be next to the definition in the dictionary.

Tim has worked in the business world, he teaches art at the middle school and high school level, possesses a master's degree, is a Command Sergeant Major (CSM) in the U.S. Army, and is a husband and father.

Coming out of high school, Tim readily admits that he didn't really have to work hard for anything while he was young and that he wasn't very disciplined. Those habits followed him to college. He didn't put much effort into his studies and was just coasting along, and he dropped out after the first year.

> *I didn't even know what discipline looked like, actually. I have always been interested in the Army, and a couple of buddies had enlisted. I have always loved history, learning about WWII, stuff like that. Once I dropped out, I had to do something, so I joined the Army. And . . . I needed the money. [Chuckles.]*

He was quickly introduced to discipline. "From moment one," he said.

> *Basic training is discipline. I didn't understand at the beginning. I just thought that these people were just really angry. Right? They break you down to your core being and then build you back up into a team. You learn to think about your "battle buddy" and the other people in your section, squad, team, or whatever. Because you can't do anything or succeed in the military alone.*

If you have heard anything about basic training in the military, you know that enlistees will undergo physical challenges like they have never seen before. Enlistees are also introduced to mental discipline.

> *What's funny is that I struggled more with the mental stuff than the physical demands. I learned how to push through when I thought that I couldn't do something. On the other hand, l learned to not think too highly of myself.*

Things dramatically changed after Tim had a powerful conversation with one of his superiors.

> *A bunch of my buddies had been promoted, and I asked him when I was going to be promoted. He just looked at me and said, "Are you kidding me? When you pull your head out of your butt long enough to see what you're doing. Then you will be promoted." He laid it all out in front of me, and I was like,* Wow, he's right. I have done all these things. *I needed to grow up and put discipline into practice. I started making*

changes in my decision-making and how I approached things. Things like being respectful before demanding respect. Being responsible for my own actions. Owning who I am and what I do. You can be different, but just own it. If you do something wrong, then apologize and move on. Just own it.

The biggest life change happened when I changed my mentality, and I was promoted the next year. And now years later, I'm a Command Sergeant Major.[1] You don't know what you don't know. I needed somebody to share it with me, and not in a nice way. Kind of get up in my face and explain it to me. I think a lot of times people are not willing to say the hard things. You don't have to be ugly about it. I think that we try to be politically correct so many times. Sometimes, you need someone to look you in the eye and tell you the truth.

Tim was deployed to Afghanistan from April 2009 to February 2010. During the first five months that he was in-country, he patrolled on foot every day. Some days, the temperature reached over 130 degrees.

It was brutal. The smell. The heat. It was just horrible.

Oh yeah, and the enemy was trying to kill him.

When I asked him how he got through it, he responded,

You understand that every day is special, and you don't look to tomorrow. You just deal with today. It's a biblical concept—"give us this day our daily

> *bread." All that I need to focus on is today and not worry about tomorrow. Tomorrow is not guaranteed and will have enough stressors of its own. Sometimes I think that we all fight too much for tomorrow and forget about living for today.*

Each day was hard, but some stood out. A couple of his friends were killed by an improvised explosive device (IED) while they were on patrol one day.

> *The next day, I was wondering if today was going to be my day. But I'm going to do my job. You buckle up, say a quick prayer, and roll out of the gate. We have a saying in the Army—just suck it up and drive on.*

During the time of his deployment, Tim held the rank of First Sergeant. He was responsible for putting his people in a position and equipping them to thrive in that environment. His experiences and responsibilities continued to increase in size and scope, and he kept getting promoted, leading up to his current rank of Command Sergeant Major.

The leadership lessons that he learned along the way are priceless and apply to almost all environments where people are involved.

> *The Army values emphasize doing your duty, honor, integrity, and respect. They apply in any situation. Focus on those things, and success will come when it comes. Don't force it.*

As people rise in responsibility and become accountable for the performance of others, their leadership traits become more apparent—whether they are good or bad. Tim reminded me that no leader in history, especially in the Army, was successful by leading from behind their desk. A true leader must see and experience the things his or her team is facing.

> *Leadership is influence. The definition of influence is to provide purpose, direction, and motivation. What are we doing, why are we doing it, and what is the end goal? Once that is explained, put your team in the best position to succeed. Empower them to do their jobs. Treat them with respect. Fight the battle of providing all the things they need to do their job . . . and then, GET OUT OF THE WAY because you can get too involved. They will start to rely on you to impact things if you are too involved. They will focus on you instead of the task at hand. I want to be the problem solver and not the problem creator. You need to be visible but just not all the time. Pick your spots.*

Wouldn't it be refreshing (and more productive) if those in charge led in this way? Blunt honesty. No egos. No office politics or agendas. No micromanaging. Nothing but the end goal in mind. I don't know who first said this, but it is so true: amazing things will happen when people aren't concerned with who gets the credit. "Selfless service" is how he summed it.

> *The love to serve others. That's the definition of Jesus, but it's also the definition of a good leader.*

Tim also mentioned something that he consistently observes as an art teacher. He is gifted in sculpting and instructs that form of art in his classes. Each project begins as a lump of clay. The student then takes that lump of clay and molds it/ chisels it/decorates it into the finished piece. He notices that his students almost always hesitate at the beginning.

> *People are afraid to make mistakes. They think that they don't really know how to start. They don't want to mess it up, so they just freeze. If you never start, then you never finish and will never know how your finished project turns out. It's OK to make a mistake. If you make a mistake, start adjusting. Learn and grow and become better. If you don't start, then you'll just sit there forever. Once you start, then confidence grows, and momentum takes over.*

He didn't emphasize this when he told me about his art students, but Tim provided a powerful lesson that we should all apply when facing a task, project, challenge, or "bump" that comes our way. *Just start.* Don't just think about it. Don't stress over it and overanalyze the situation. Act on it.

My uncle would often say, "Do *something* even if it's wrong." If we never start, then we will never finish.

> » **Selfless service is the best way to lead.**
>
> » **Take complete ownership of your actions.**
>
> » **Just start. Do your job. Be fearless. Don't be afraid to make a mistake.**

BARRY

W hen I was doing research for this little project, I came across a list of the top causes of stress in life. Divorce, facing a major illness, and the loss of a job are among the leading causes. Barry's life checked every box. Adding to the "fun," he experienced all these life events in a very short timeframe—all happened over three consecutive years.

Anger.

Uncertainty.

Fear of the unknown.

Doubt.

Frustration.

> *Yep, I've been through some major stuff. I've had cancer twice, job loss, divorce, you name it. You know, all it did was prepare me to manage things and to do more and more and more.*

Lessons that he learned growing up provided a blueprint of how to handle tough situations.

My dad was a lifelong polio survivor, and I saw how he dealt with things. He never let anything get him down. He always kept a positive attitude and learned to find the blessings in every situation—good or bad. Never complained. He had every right to complain, but he never did. You can look at things and find something good that's going to come out of it. That role model really helped when I was going through everything. Sure. I was blessed with that.

Barry added a familiar saying:

Don't sweat the small stuff.

Everyone has two major decisions to make when they wake up in the morning. They can decide whether it is going to be a great day or a lousy day. The choice is up to us.

It isn't easy to do, and it takes a lot of energy and focus to stay positive when you're deep into it. But again, I was always trying to stay positive no matter what. Look at it from my kids' perspective. Early in 2003, our kids' grandfather (my ex-wife's father) was in hospice in our house with pancreatic cancer, and he died. I didn't want my kids to think cancer equals death, so I portrayed "normal" the best as possible during my cancer diagnosis in 2012. I made their lunches. I visited them at their school. When they weren't at home, that's when I would sit down and suffer. What else could I do? I didn't want them to see that. So again, it gets back to the image you want to put out there and your belief in positivity.

Barry counsels a lot of people soon after they have been diagnosed with the disease.

> *We will take a walk and talk about things. All that I do is listen. Just listen, and then tell him or her that it's OK to be mad/sad/scared/ confused/whatever. Go ahead and ask the "why me?" question. Have the pity party. Feel sorry for yourself. But at some point, you've got to flip that switch and change your attitude. Once you do that, you're going to find that your life is so much more fulfilling, and you will be better prepared to manage and deal with what's about to happen. You don't know what's going to happen—the treatment, how you're going to feel, how people react to you having cancer, all that stuff. It's hard. It's a pain. It's difficult. When you're not feeling well and being negative about everything, people aren't going to want to be around you anyway, right? But the more you adjust your attitude to the positive and the quicker you do it; the better you're going to be able to manage and deal with everything, including the people around you.*

Like a lot of things, staying positive is easier said than done. Barry told me about a major meltdown that he experienced and what turned it around.

> *I was sitting in a parking lot one morning and didn't know what to do with everything going on. I had no idea. I'm trying to figure it all out. So I called a mutual friend of ours, wanting to hear, "Oh, I'm so sorry," or, "That must be terrible"—you know, kind of treat me with kid*

gloves. Instead, he rips me a new one. He told me very plainly and very directly that I need to get my act together and man-up. It's nice to hear what you want to hear, but sometimes you need another point of view said strongly, and you need to hear it strongly. He could express it in that way because we are close friends. Sometimes you need friends like that. I credit him for getting things turned in the right direction for me.

While he was in college, Barry raced bicycles. He played college football and got into cycling when his football days came to an end, and he needed to lose some weight. A friend of his introduced him to the velodrome—a track made specifically for cycling—and success soon followed. He was winning on a regular basis and moved out to Colorado to race full time. Because cycling is not an inexpensive activity, and his student loans came due, his bank account soon ran dry. So he moved back to the South and returned to *reality*.

Barry entered the working world, eventually got married, had kids, gained ninety pounds, and gave up cycling altogether. Then, he hit some "bumps" and "potholes." *Cancer. Divorce. Job loss. Savings depleted due to the cancer treatment.*

Oh yeah, throw a pandemic into the mix.

He had battled through everything and was coming out of the blur of some very serious life events . . . and the pandemic hits! C'mon, seriously?

Well, the pandemic turned out to be a blessing for Barry. He was living in a remote area in the North Carolina mountains and used the down time to start working on his own health. His business-related travel was shut down completely, so after his Zoom calls were finished for the day, he made time to hike, kayak, and ride. Barry drastically changed his diet, getting to the point where he now only eats plant-based food. He has since lost ninety pounds.

> *Then I thought that I might be able to race again. I also have a passion for skiing. I'm thinking that the best place to do both things is in Colorado, and here I am.*

Soon after Barry moved back to Colorado, he joined a bike club and trains with them to this day. He is racing again.

The way that he lost weight by altering his diet has gained him some notoriety.

> *People ask me all the time for advice on weight loss and diet. The quality of food that you put into your body helps you perform and recover. Everyone is different. You don't have to go to all plant-based food like me. It works for me. If you like chicken, beef, or pork, then eat a better quality of those foods. Also, make them a smaller portion of your meal. The biggest thing that works for everyone is to add more color to your plate and eat more vegetables.*

Life is rolling along smoothly for Barry now. He worked his way through the "bumps." There is a great chance that his now-adult kids will soon end up living near him so they can all be together more often. He has knocked on the door of his goal of reaching a podium at the USA Masters Track Nationals and then reaching the World Championships in Manchester England. (He is so close!)

Prayer has always been a large part of his daily routine. Through prayer comes patience.

Sometimes the answer to prayers is not exactly what we ask for, or things don't happen as quickly as we want. We want immediate or at least soon. It doesn't happen like that.

Believe it or not, Barry is thankful that he faced these "bumps." He turned them into opportunities.

I'm not going to deny that it wasn't painful going through all of this. It was. It stunk. But it was the best thing that ever happened to me. It taught me to look at life through a different set of lenses.

Things are good. I am blessed to have each morning.

» **Sometimes blunt honesty is the best.**

» **We have two choices when we wake up each day—we can expect a great day or a lousy day. We get to make that choice.**

» **Learn to find the blessings in every situation—good *and* bad.**

TOM

Whether we like it or not, social media is here to stay. It is used to connect or reconnect with potential business associates, friends, and family members. You can find people with common interests to discuss and dig deeper into that activity. We get to see the meal that people are about to ingest, photos of their cat, examples of their riches and fame, and how perfect their life is . . . yes, it does have its annoying aspects. Social media is also used by keyboard cowboys to bully, brag, threaten, and make uninvited comments in an anonymous way.

Social media can be a cesspool. People comment in ways they never would if they were face-to-face with you. It can be nasty. Vicious. Hurtful. Vulgar.

But it can be pretty dang cool.

When I was a little kid, my best friend and his two older brothers and sister lived in the neighborhood house where everything happened. It was a magnet for kids. Epic football and baseball games were played in the front yard. We made ramps and jumped them with our bikes (think a mini Evel Knievel on a Schwinn Stingray bicycle). When we got hot and thirsty in the Georgia summers, we would either line up and drink water straight out of the garden hose or go inside and grab a popsicle from the freezer. We played and did all the things that were typical of kids who grew up in the late 1960s and 1970s.

Since my buddy was the youngest sibling, I got to know some of the friends of his older brothers and sister. My buddy and I were the tag-alongs to the big kids. Tom was one of the big kids.

He and I went to the same elementary and high school. Tom was a member of the class that graduated two years ahead of me (he was a senior when I was a tenth grader). It turns out that we both graduated from the same university, but we lost touch during high school.

Tom matured before I did. He got his driver's license a few years before I started driving. Our interests changed. It's normal.

Decades passed by. My kids were now in college, and they both ended up attending Mississippi State University in Starkville, MS.

I was fiddling around on Facebook one day, and Tom appeared on the "People You May Know" section of my page. I learned that he now lives in Meridian, MS, about one and a half hours away from Starkville. To make a somewhat long story short, we reconnected and now talk/text/message each other on a regular basis. His adult son, Tommy, owns a marketing agency[2] and built a business website for me. Now that is pretty stinking cool. All made possible by social media!

Tom is a pastor in Meridian[3] and is dedicated to making a difference in his community. In addition to his daily actions and through his role at the church, he serves others through various mission trips and his non-profit organizations.[4]

The special needs community is one area that he is passionate about.

The whole family system involved in a special needs situation is really isolated, especially since Covid hit. The person with special needs, their parents, family members, everyone involved.

Isolation and exhaustion are the two main factors faced by those in a special needs situation. The entire support system is affected. For example, do the parents choose to get out of the house and go to a restaurant for a meal? If they do, then there might be a distraction. How are people going to react? Are other people going to act kindly or rudely? More times than not, the parents will choose to stay home and avoid the situation altogether and remain isolated from others.

What I have found is that the special needs community is starving for fellowship. They want to be around other people. The kids want to be kids, and the parents want to have "normal" conversations and let their guard down for a little bit.

To help with this, Tom is heavily involved with a non-profit organization created specifically to be a local gathering place and resource for families with special needs children. Named The SPOT (Special Place for Others to Thrive),[5] this organization provides a one-stop, online resource for parents and caregivers that lists local agencies, therapists, and support groups that cater to the special needs community. The SPOT also provides a brick-and-mortar location for families to get together and enjoy each other's company.

Organizations such as The SPOT are designed to smooth out the "bumps" encountered by people involved in that community.

Tom went through a not-so-smooth time in his life when he was going down the road to becoming a pastor. His father was the only veterinarian in America to ever become a state epidemiologist. He worked at the Center for Disease Control (CDC) and developed the rabies vaccine that is used today. Growing up, Tom's world revolved around medicine.

> *That's all I ever heard, and I wanted to be a doctor when I grew up. My dad was so happy. I was the youngest of three brothers and I was the last hope that my dad had for one of his sons to follow in his footsteps.*

Tom began his college career majoring in pre-med, but something happened along the way. He didn't finish in that area of study. One summer he went on a mission trip and witnessed a degree of love and selfless service that he had never seen before. It moved his heart and his mind. Experiencing the things that he did on that trip and through a relationship he had with a chaplain at his school, Tom was introduced to a model of ministry that he really enjoyed and admired. Tom was feeling the tug to go into ministry.

> *When I told my dad that I was going to stop studying medicine and wanted to become a minister, well, that didn't go too well. I knew I was doing the right thing. He didn't think so.*

The two basically became estranged over the situation. They didn't talk for two years. Tom finished his undergraduate degree and paid his own way through graduate school and seminary. It wasn't easy for him, but it does have a happy ending.

> *My dad finally came around when he heard me preach a sermon. He came up to me afterwards and told me that I had found my calling.*

By sticking to his vision and following his heart, Tom was able to navigate through the "bumps" that he encountered on his way to pursuing his profession.

Since then, he has helped people find peace, hope, and purpose for more than thirty years.

> » **There is power in a community of close relationships.**

> » **Follow your heart.**

> » **Be generous. Be appreciative. Be humble.**

PHIL

P hil has firsthand knowledge of the isolation, frustration, and exhaustion felt by those in the special needs and developmentally disabled community. He is knee-deep in it every day.

His son, Evan, had an accident at home when he was one and a half years old that caused severe trauma to his brain.

> *He fell and hit his head. All little kids fall, and there wasn't any blood or bruising, so we thought nothing of it. He woke up the following day extremely cranky and fussy, and we just thought that he might have the flu because it was going around in our family.*

When they went to get him up from his nap later that day, he didn't budge. He was unresponsive. *He wasn't waking up.* They called 911 and Evan was rushed to the hospital. The medical staff found that he had suffered general trauma to the brain. An emergency craniotomy was performed, and they found that twenty percent of his brain had been severely damaged. Evan stayed in the ICU for five weeks.

It turned our world upside down. We were devastated.

Those events happened over twenty years ago. Since then, Phil and his family have had to help Evan with the daily activities of life that most of us take for granted—dressing, toileting, feeding, shaving, bathing, etc. He will need assistance with those activities for the rest of his life. Evan's physical body reflects his twenty-one years of age, but he has the mental non-verbal equivalencies of a three-year-old.

Evan is in the three percent of the population that have what is termed *intellectual and developmental disabilities* (IDD). These are acquired or at-birth disabilities that include Down syndrome and autism.

Without a trace of bitterness, Phil confirmed the isolation and exhaustion experienced in the IDD community. He told me that large public events such as concerts or athletic games are often avoided due to the over-stimulation (sounds, lighting, etc.) that would affect the person with IDD. The venue may not be set up to handle IDD situations—most places do not have family restrooms, easy in-and-out parking, etc.

Taking him out in public is work. He can never be out of line of site from me because he has no safety awareness. It's constant stress and it wears you down.

Phil shared that IDD parents will lose friends along the way, adding to the isolation. Some people do not know what to say or how to react, and they just disappear. They don't know how to handle all the added distractions, so they remove themselves from the situation.

I go out of my way to get Evan out in the community. But it's not easy.

As we age, we don't have the energy that we once had. We don't bounce around from one activity to another as easily as we did in our younger years. This is obvious. Caretakers wear down just like anyone else, and their responsibilities don't stop at bedtime.

Getting a full night of uninterrupted sleep is like finding gold. [Chuckles.] I get one every now and then and really appreciate it.

Planning for the future can be a moving target and another cause of stress for parents of a child with special needs. What happens when the parent ages and needs assistance or is no longer there? Who is going to take care of their child, love on them, and make sure that they have a great quality of life?

Phil found that the options are not great. The public education system will host children with special needs until they age out of the program when they reach twenty-two years of age. Parents will then need to find some sort of day program so they can go to work. Those can cost twenty-to-twenty-five thousand dollars a year. If the person with IDD moves into a residential living situation, those arrangements cost as much as assisted living communities—it's not cheap. Put all of that together over a span of twenty, thirty, or forty years, and it takes a lot of money. A lot of money. Millions of *after-tax* dollars.

One option to avoid these lofty costs is to send the now-adult developmentally disabled individual to a tax-funded group home or institution. Largely a result of the inability to find qualified caretakers who are willing to work for not-so-great wages, these arrangements commonly house ten or so individuals.

Is this a good fit? Is the quality of life provided in this type of situation what you want for your child?

Along the way to raising and caring for Evan, Phil and his wife, Lisa, have become advocates for the IDD community. In 1999, a Supreme Court ruling paved a way to move IDD individuals out of institutions and put them into a home community setting. This situation improves the quality of life of IDD residents and is less expensive than tax-funded institutions. The ruling basically states that intellectually and developmentally disabled individuals have a right to live in the community, and their care can be funded by the states through a Medicaid waiver. This can be done *if* the state of residence allocates the money. Some states do. Some states don't.

Phil and Lisa have become advocates in their home state of Georgia along their IDD journey. When they first became involved in the legislative process, they discovered that the state was fully funding waivers for approximately one hundred individuals per year. Through their combined efforts with others to raise the visibility of the situation, the state recently increased funding for an additional 413 families. That's fantastic and will literally change the lives of those families! However, there are still approximately seven thousand families in Georgia that are enduring the IDD experience. At least sixty-five hundred families could be helped by this waiver if/when the funds are made available.

Bringing attention to and impacting the IDD community has its own set of unique challenges. For one, it only affects three percent of the overall population—so people might only *hear* about an IDD situation versus having a personal tie to it. It's also difficult to organize this community because of the nature of the situation. You will not see a large gathering of intellectually and developmentally disabled kids raising a ruckus, banging on drums, chanting clever phrases, and marching in parades in front of the bright lights of the local media.

Ain't gonna happen.

Parents find it difficult to get together because if they are at a meeting to talk about bringing visibility to the situation, who is caring for their child during that time? Remember, there is a shortage of qualified caretakers.

It is challenging all the way around. Phil, Lisa, and Evan will continue to walk the halls of the state Capitol to talk with lawmakers and participate in activities to help the situation.

We are going to continue that fight.

Obviously Phil has endured a lot of ups and downs in the years following Evan's accident. I asked him how he has been able to manage all the physical and mental challenges that he has faced along the way, and he shared that he was an atheist—or at least an agnostic—before Evan's accident. He attended church to give his kids a moral foundation. He even taught Sunday school, but he didn't believe in Jesus. Then Evan had his accident.

> *I was desperate for anything that could help my son and started reading the Bible and highlighting every place that Jesus healed somebody. That triggered my interest and curiosity about the Bible, and reading it became a regular thing. My faith and reliance on Jesus started growing and continues to grow. That's where I find strength.*

37

Phil mentioned this one specific incident:

> *When his accident first happened, Evan was having like a dozen seizures each day. Our doctor told us that he is regressing into severe retardation leading to death. How does that make you feel as a parent, right? We were sitting at the dinner table one night about to say grace. Usually Evan couldn't sit still for more than ten minutes at a time, and we would take turns keeping him seated. He never recognized or acknowledged anything spiritual. He just sat there during the prayer . . . if he sat. So we are sitting at the table, and he puts his little hands up to his eyes in a "prayer pose" and sits quietly through grace. And it was a good one . . . like a minute long. My wife, daughter, and I saw this and thought,* Holy cow, look at this. *He had no seizures the following day and hasn't had one since! When people say that miracles don't happen, dude, I saw if firsthand! It was one of those things that just really builds your faith.*

Parents make a lot of sacrifices for their children. Some delay opportunities for work advancement so they can coach their kids' sports team. Others work multiple jobs so they can set aside money for their children's plans after high school.

Parents of children with special needs have their own set of sacrifices, and the reason behind everything is universal.

We do all of this because we love our kids.

When you see a special needs family out and about, make the effort to acknowledge them. Both the parent *and* the child. They deserve a nod and a friendly smile.

» Treat *all* people with respect and dignity.

» Help those who can't help themselves.

» Be kind. We have no idea what others are going through.

SHANE AND JULIE

I first met Shane and Julie through the "Young Marrieds" Sunday school class at the church that my wife and I attended. We were all around the same age, had been married for the same amount of time, had common interests, and were going through the same stages of life.

Julie was one of the "Bunco Babes"—the group of gals that got together each month to play this dicey game—and spent time at our house when it was my wife's turn to host.

Shane was a friend to all. Everyone who met him liked him. He was very kind and compassionate, and he always thought the best of people. He was a true servant leader who took great pleasure in helping people in all areas of his life.

We have been friends for a long time.

Shane and Julie went through a situation that nobody would envy. The two were painting their garage one muggy summer evening, and Shane noticed a hard spot on his neck after he wiped the sweat off his face and neck. He initially didn't think much of it but eventually had it checked out when it didn't go away.

The lump was a cancerous mass.

Once the initial shock of the diagnosis wore off, he started an intense treatment program that included radiation and chemo. All at the same time. And it was awful. I have had cancer patients tell me that if the cancer doesn't kill you, the treatment will. But undergoing the aggressive treatment protocol was working. Shane was in remission for around three and a half years.

Shane was at a point where his doctor moved him from a six-month checkup to yearly scans to see if the disease had returned. Unfortunately it did. And it returned with a vengeance. It was annoying and painful and drained every ounce of energy from his body. The life expectancy for people with this form of cancer under these circumstances was three years.

Shane willingly and intentionally underwent new treatments and participated in different trials. Julie told me that Shane felt strongly about trying new therapies because it might help others even if it doesn't help him.

Throughout Shane's second bout with cancer, he and Julie both had a common desire. They consistently prayed that this experience would make their faith, and the faith of their girls, stronger and that their cancer journey would constantly point people toward God.

Shane would often say,

> *S: I know that I'll be fully healed—it just may not be here on this earth.*

Shane succumbed to this awful disease two years after the cancer returned.

> *J: His faith in God gave him peace, and he died the most peaceful death.*

Ever since I've known her, Julie always has a smile on her face and is full of joy. She handled Shane's passing with extreme grace and composure. It wasn't easy. She grieved. She cried. She got mad at the situation. Julie admits that there were times when she just wanted to curl up in a ball and hide, hoping that everything would go away.

The fact that Shane lived his life with no regrets helped Julie and her daughters get through this situation.

> *J: He didn't leave any unfinished business and would tell me that everything was going to be fine.*

Shane knew that Julie and the girls would receive a ton of support from their church, friends, and family. And they have.

> *J: It would have broken Shane's heart if we just broke down and stopped. I need to be strong for my girls, right? They are watching. And I try, but it doesn't mean that I don't have bad days.*

As a parent, Julie has been and continues to be very *real* with her daughters and encourages them to be *real* with her.

> *J: I'll tell them that this is hard. This sucks. That I couldn't imagine what it's like to lose your dad as a teenager. I would say that it's OK to get mad at God and that this isn't fair. God can take it.*

Julie told her girls that we all have a choice every day of how we look at things and that attitude is extremely important.

She explained that things may not look like we expect them to but that God is never going to leave us.

> *J: When you pray or ask God for help, you're not rubbing on the genie bottle. You are not going to get an immediate answer to your three wishes. No, it doesn't work like that. We can't control or choose what is going to happen to us, but we can choose how we react to it. Are we going to be a victim of our circumstances, or are we going to overcome our circumstances and use them to make us stronger? We have that choice!*

Julie shared how the whole cancer thing was handled with her daughters.

> *J: After the initial diagnosis, Shane and I asked the girls (who were teenagers at the time) if they wanted to know details along the way, or if they wanted to be spared with that. They wanted to know everything, so we let them drive the conversations and told them as much as they wanted to know.*

Despite the difficult circumstances, Julie still flashes that smile and finds humor in almost every situation. We both agreed that very well-meaning people will say some very inappropriate things in some of the most difficult moments. They are trying to help, but it comes out wrong.

Either that, or they are just dense.

> *J: Early on in our journey, when Shane had just started his treatments, we were talking with this one guy, and he asked me if I had picked out my next husband. You've got to be kidding! Really?*

Shane and I looked at each other to see if we really heard what we thought we heard. And we did.

The two laughed all the way home.

J: *I mean, c'mon, that's funny. Kind of rude, but funny.*

» **Every day is special.**

» **Are we going to be a victim of our circumstances, or are we going to overcome our circumstances and use them to make us stronger? We have that choice.**

» **Find humor in every situation.**

EDDIE, BECKY, AND KNOX

F or those of us that were born after the year 2000, we experienced—in one form or another—the fallout of the financial crisis and global recession that occurred between 2007 and 2010.

Close to nine million jobs in the United States were lost during 2008 and 2009. Underemployment, if not unemployment, was common.

U.S. household net worth declined by nearly $13 trillion from its pre-recession peak in 2007.

Savings accounts . . . if we had any . . . shrunk in size. Our 401(k)s became 201(k)s.

I vividly remember driving through a subdivision and seeing furniture, clothing, a television set, and children's toys heaped in a pile on the street. This family had lost their house because of a foreclosure.

Eddie was one of many who felt the pain of the recession. He is one of those highly skilled individuals who can take a bare plot of land and transform it into an elegant place to live. From pouring the foundation, wiring the electricity, and installing the plumbing and drywall, to hammering out the actual construction of the house—he can do it all.

That was how he made his living. Until the recession hit.

Eddie was involved in buying, renovating, renting, and selling single and multi-family houses. And he was very good at it. He partnered with a few banks and, over time, grew his real estate and investment properties into a multimillion-dollar portfolio.

Then, the bubble burst and he hit a major "pothole."

At the very front end of the recession, the U.S. administration was paying eighty cents on the dollar to banks that obtained property by demanding full payment of the loan and repossessing the property when the loan couldn't be paid in full. In southern-speak, this means that the lender would "call the note" and tell the borrower to pay in full within thirty to ninety days or the property would be repo'd.

Banks were soon jumping on the government-backed guarantee bandwagon to try and minimize their losses, regardless of their prior relationship with the borrower.

In the sixteen years that Eddie worked with his banking partners, he had never missed or even been late with any payment. That didn't matter. Eddie and his wife, Becky, were told to repay the loans within ninety days or lose their properties.

Most people don't have millions of dollars in cash on hand, stuffed in their mattress or buried in the backyard (known locally as "midnight gardening"), that they can use in this type of situation. Eddie and Becky were "most people."

Paying that amount of money in that time frame under those circumstances was impossible.

They lost everything and eventually had to file for bankruptcy.

> **B:** *I've never seen a more broken sight in my life. [Said of Eddie] He did everything the right way. Paid everything on time. Treated people the right way. He worked extremely hard and was honest in everything that he did. And it still didn't work out.*

Eddie admits that he was angry and frustrated. Who wouldn't be? He did not cut any corners or venture into that *grey* area in business that separates right from wrong, honest from dishonest. He was mad at the situation. He was mad at himself. He was mad at everything and everyone, including God.

> **E:** *They don't leave you with much when you file for bankruptcy, and sitting around not working was not an option. I don't know how they found out, but the school that my kids were attending discovered that I fluently spoke French and Spanish, and they had an opening for a teacher to instruct those languages. I'm a business guy and not a teacher and wasn't sure that this was a good fit, so they let me rotate around the other language teachers for a week to get a better understanding of the position. I liked what I saw, and so I taught for a while.*

What Eddie did not fully realize when he accepted the position was that the pay scale at the school was based on tenure at the school and not overall experience. In other words, he would bring home the same dollar amount as a first-year teacher straight out of college and advance in pay at the same rate. Eddie wasn't going to be able to "fast-track" his income. He quickly understood that he wasn't going to rapidly move up on the pay scale like he could in the business world. But it was an opportunity to bring in some money at a time when he needed it.

At the time, Eddie was forty years old with a family of five. He was determined to do whatever it took to make ends meet, even if that meant working an extra job or two. Becky also landed a position at the school. For the next few years, the two of them worked as hard as possible, but they were only bringing home a fraction of what they made in the pre-recession years and living only two hundred dollars a month over the national poverty level.

Financial struggles are one of the main causes of marital problems and, ultimately, divorce in America.

Too much month left at the end of the money increases stress and shortens tempers. Eddie and Becky both admit that neither was a joy to be around during this time. Tensions were high, and life was not all that rosy. Both were trying to fix the situation, but neither could do or say the right things to make the tension go away. It was miserable.

But they were committed to making things better and grinded their way through it.

> *E: Becky and I were both working, but we were still below the poverty line. It was a daily struggle between God and me. But every month, the bills would get paid. We never had to miss a meal. We received what we needed when we needed it. It was crazy and didn't make any sense if you strictly looked at the numbers on paper.*

> *Finally, after about a year of this happening, I fell on my knees and told God that I understand that He is in charge and that He is taking care of everything. Once I did this, I quit worrying about all of it, and it took the stress away.*
>
> *I've always been a firm believer in God. Pre-bankruptcy, I would have told you that I believe that He makes everything and owns everything . . . but I earned it. Post-bankruptcy, I will tell you that I didn't earn anything. God owns everything. He oversees everything and takes care of everything.*

Eddie shared that we can't just sit around and wait for God to show up when we face difficult times. We must do our part. We need to work. We need to take that first step. We need to pray and build a relationship with Him in good *and* bad times. We need to rely on Him and trust that He will give us everything we need.

Because He will.

~*~

Eddie and Becky have three children—Knox, Riley, and Madeline. Knox is the oldest, and he was studying abroad during the summer of 2017 before beginning his junior year in college. One morning in August while Knox was in Europe, Becky woke up and noticed that she had a voicemail on her phone. The message had been transcribed, and she realized that it was from someone in Italy, which is where Knox was at the time. The voicemail said that Knox had been in an accident. Becky threw the phone to Eddie and had him check to see that she was reading the message correctly. *Is this true?*

It was.

Eddie called the person who sent the message and verified that Knox had, in fact, been in an accident, but he was alive and breathing.

Every parent fears getting a phone call in the middle of the night concerning their child. Becky received *that* phone call, and it went straight to voicemail because her phone was set to "Do Not Disturb."

She felt helpless. She couldn't get to her son. Becky couldn't hug him and do that *mom thing* to try to make the hurt go away. She began petitioning and arguing with God.

> **B:** *God, no! God, I can't get to him!*

Then she heard a little voice tell her, *I'm already there.*

Two days prior, Becky was getting ready to begin seminary and was doing some last-minute studying. This was a big deal considering her family had just come out of a financial crisis and was moving back to a single-income household. Becky decided to take a break and do some cleaning with hopes of clearing her mind.

> **B:** *I was vacuuming and listening to music, and I heard the Holy Spirit[6] tell me to pray for Knox. So I started praying for Knox while I continued to clean things with my music on.*
>
> *Then, the Holy Spirit said in a big and loud voice to stop what I was doing, get on my knees, and pray for Knox. I didn't like what I was hearing, but I'm going to be obedient. So I dropped to my knees and had this five-minute prayer, asking for Knox's safety and protection*

*and that he would be a godly influence on his
friends.*

Remembering this encounter from a few days prior, she knew
somehow, someway, that Knox was going to be OK.

The reason for the middle-of-the-night phone call was to tell
her that Knox had experienced a seizure while he was in Italy.
When he returned home, Becky took Knox to a neurologist for
testing to make sure that everything was fine. After seeing the
doctor and nurses, they were told that someone from the office
would call them in a couple of weeks with the test results. As
Becky and Knox were leaving, a nurse stopped them and told
the two that the doctor would like to talk with them.

Well, this can't be good, Becky thought.

Becky and Knox sat down in the doctor's office. The doctor
patted Becky's hands and told them that she had arranged for
them to see a surgeon that day for further testing.

Wonderful.

After the surgeon had completed her testing, she matter-of-
factly broke the news that Knox had a large growth in his
brain that needed to be removed within a week. Pathology
would later confirm that Knox had an anaplastic astrocytoma,
an aggressive form of brain cancer that can progress to a
Glioblastoma (GBM). The relative five-year survival rate of
patients diagnosed with GBM is only 7.2%, and the median
survival span is only eight months.

There wasn't time to freak out—just focus to move forward
and find a neurosurgeon that could perform the procedure
ASAP. Becky and Knox felt strongly about this being
performed in partnership with a research hospital, and Becky
began networking to find a neurosurgeon.

53

Upon a recommendation from a friend, Becky contacted one of the world's best surgeons in this field, Dr. Keith Black. His office was in Los Angeles, and they lived in Georgia.

Not exactly convenient.

Dr. Black's office responded within a day and asked how quickly they could get there. The response was,

> **B:** *How about tomorrow?*

It just so happened that Becky's sister lived in Los Angeles and had a place for them to stay. Becky states that "just so happened" was not true; it was a "God thing."

The procedure was done within a week of Knox's initial diagnosis. He endured multiple rounds of chemotherapy and radiation over the next several months while they were in California. His dad (Eddie), brother, and sister would fly in from Georgia and visit as often as possible.

Knox fought. And fought. And fought. He fought it in California, at Duke Medical Center in North Carolina, and at home in Georgia.

Becky was always by his side, protecting, nurturing, encouraging, and coaching him through this awful ordeal.

Over the next three years while Knox battled this ugly disease, he continued to live his life to the fullest. He was a typical college kid—who happened to have a terrible form of brain cancer. He was an active, proud member of Phi Gamma Delta fraternity at the University of Georgia (UGA). He loved attending football games in the fall and cheering on the Dawgs at Sanford Stadium. Knox enjoyed camping and being outdoors.

Knox graduated from UGA, lived independently with close friends, and was working in the "real" world. He was doing all kinds of things that most people who have a severe form of brain cancer don't get to do.

He had a high quality of life until he didn't. Knox succumbed to this horrific disease on December 1, 2020. He was twenty-four years old.

~*~

We never envision burying our children. When Grandma, Grandpa, Mom, or Dad pass away, it is very sad, but it is somewhat expected in the genealogy of things. We do not expect to go to a funeral for someone younger than us—especially conducting and attending a funeral for our own child.

I asked Eddie and Becky how they were able to even function after going through this jarring ordeal. Without hesitating, they both told me that God had prepared them in their situation with bankruptcy. Becky compared it to Navy SEAL training where you become stronger when you experience overwhelming and challenging situations.

Most people struggle with why things happen to "good" people.

> *E: I had already been through all of that. I had no more anger to dish out. I had already been through the fighting and struggling. It helped me accept the fact that life just happens. We don't get to control who dies, when they die, how they die, or what order they die in. It's going to happen to us all eventually.*

B: God was telling us that he has already equipped us and that He is going to fight for us and with us. We could curl up in a corner . . . and nobody would probably think any less of us . . . but who would we be giving the power to if we did this? We'd be giving the power to the enemy, right? God is telling us to stand up and face this thing—not with our power but with His power. God was telling me to get myself in a place where I can advocate for my son.

It was not going to be a pity party. I had done that for a really long time, and I realized that no fruit ever came from that. Nothing good came from feeling sorry for myself.

E: God has taken care of us for so long, and He is helping us through this.

In December of 2022, Becky received her post-graduate degree from Emory University's Candler School of Theology. But instead of becoming an ordained minister, she changed her focus of study to a program in non-profit leadership based on a theological perspective. Forged from her unique life experiences combined with the things she learned in her graduate program, Becky became CEO of the Knox Martin Foundation for Brain Cancer Research[7] four months after Knox's passing.

Unfortunately, the speed and lethality of Knox's cancer are the underlying causes for why research studies and treatments for Glioblastoma are so low compared to the funding for other forms of cancer. GBM outcomes are poor because there are very few research studies conducted, and there are so few research studies conducted because the outcomes are so poor. It takes on the form of "which came first, the chicken or the egg?" The Knox Martin Foundation for Brain Cancer Research (KMF) wants to change that scenario. The mission of this 501c3 non-profit organization is to fund research for aggressive brain cancers, particularly Glioblastoma, so that a diagnosis becomes widely treatable and curable.

As of the time of this writing, KMF has partnered with the Preston Robert Tisch Brain Center at Duke University, has raised over $600,000, and has funded two new FDA-approved clinical trials to advance the treatment of this disease.

» **Build a relationship with God and rely on Him in good *and* bad times.**

» **Surrender. We are not in charge.**

» **Use your gifts and experiences to be an advocate for others.**

BROOKLYNN

O ne of the two most common things that I have heard
in conducting research for this little book is the
importance of having a positive mindset when facing the
"bumps" and "potholes" in life. Everyone I have spoken with
has mentioned how immensely it helped them.

The concept of positivity is nothing new.

When I was a young salesman, Zig Ziglar[8] was *the man* when
it came to motivating people—especially businesspeople.
During his lifetime, Zig influenced and encouraged
millions through his books, audio messages (cassettes/CDs/
downloads), and live interactions. His sincere, folksy, and
funny teachings all centered around the power of what we
put in our mind and how that affects our daily lives and
individual performance.

One of his quotes that has stuck with me over the years is
this: "We all need a daily checkup from the neck up to avoid
stinkin' thinkin', which ultimately leads to hardening of the
attitudes."

Countless books have been written, careers have been
launched, and fame has been formed by people touting the

benefits of deliberately thinking and acting from a positive mindset. This subject is a multi-million-dollar industry.

Positive thinking—how we interpret and approach circumstances—is a biblical concept. The Bible, the best "self-help" document ever written, tells us that our actions flow directly from what is in our heart and mind and that we must be extremely careful about what we let in.

Garbage in = garbage out.

Our brain is a busy place. We see something or something happens to us, and we have a thought. Someone cuts in front of us in traffic, and we have a thought. We walk by a mirror and that triggers a thought. We are about to go into an appointment, and a new thought pops into our mind. And on and on and on.

There is no definitive answer on the number of thoughts that our brain processes each day, but it has been widely reported that we have anywhere from sixty-two hundred to sixty thousand thoughts per day.

Eighty percent of those thoughts are negative, glass half-empty thoughts.

Ninety-five percent of those thoughts are repetitive. That's ninety-five percent recycled, deeply engrained, *Groundhog Day* thoughts. Only five percent are new and original.

Researchers at Queen's University in Canada established a method that can detect the beginning and the end of a thought.[9] They collected data using MRI scans from 184 volunteers and were able to detect when the brain shifted from one thought to the next. Assuming the volunteers averaged eight hours of sleep each night, the researchers concluded that everyone has approximately sixty-two hundred thoughts per day.

Regardless of whether we produce sixty-two hundred, twelve thousand, or sixty thousand, there's a whole lot of thinking going on inside of us.

To err on the low side of the findings, let's agree that we produce sixty-two hundred thoughts per day. Eighty percent of those thoughts have been determined to be negative. If my math is correct, that means that we think 4,960 negative thoughts every single day.

Imagine how different things would be if we changed those negative thoughts into positive thoughts. Do you think it would make us better husbands, wives, parents, employees, patients, bosses, friends, students, sons, or daughters? If we were able to change just half of those 4,960 negative thoughts into positive thoughts, that leaves us with 2,480 negative thoughts and 3,720 positive thoughts per day. It swings the pendulum and tips the seesaw to our advantage. The positives now outweigh the negatives. This seems a whole lot better than exhausting ourselves swimming against the current of negativity each day.

Is it possible to impact our thought process? Can we influence how we think?

Absolutely!

While I was still pondering whether to dive into this project (I thought about this for more than six years before getting serious about it and acting on the idea), I heard a timely, interesting, and thought-provoking message one Sunday morning. This is normal, in case any of the church staff is reading this (ha!). Brooklynn Warren, the engagement and guest services director at Gwinnett Church in Sugar Hill, GA, spoke that summer day as part of a series called "Mind Shift."[10] Her lesson focused on the power of what goes into our mind, how we can impact our thoughts, and how the Apostle Paul addressed this in the Bible. The way she presented everything was incredible!

Brooklynn spoke about neuroplasticity, which is the brain's ability to evolve and adapt in response to life experiences. In other words, neuroplasticity allows us to retrain our brains and form new thought patterns.

Brooklynn explained that we need to recognize those negative thoughts, capture them, destroy them, and replace them with positive thoughts. And do this over and over. This is not a "one and done" activity. This must be done consistently and with intention.

I mentioned earlier that one of the top two most common traits among the people that I spoke with while doing research for this book was *positivity*. The other trait is *faith*. The people I interviewed all have a strong faith. They have a biblical faith where they have complete trust in something they cannot see.

In her lesson that day, Brooklynn talked about the Apostle Paul's second letter to the Corinthians (2 Corinthians 10:3-5) where Paul writes about our need to keep focus and that we have divine weapons—powered by God—that help us demolish the things that are preventing us from living our best lives. These weapons—the Word of God in the Spirit of God—have the power to demolish the strongholds that hold us back.

What is the main factor that takes us off course to where we want to go and leads us to a place of defeat and pain?

The answer is how we view things. Our mindset. Negative thoughts.

Brooklynn explained in her own unique way that the Apostle Paul is telling us that if we want to transform our lives, we must begin by renewing our mind.

> *You need to recognize those bad thoughts, take them captive, and destroy them, and replace them with positive thoughts . . . thoughts that are from God's Word. This is the process of renewing our mind, and we need to do it over and over again.*

One method of replacing those negative thoughts is by placing sticky notes in highly visible places where the negative thoughts tend to pop up. Brooklynn suggested putting them in places such as on our computer screen, the mirror in the bathroom, the lock screen on our smartphone, near the coffee maker, on the fridge, and on the dashboard in our car. On these sticky notes, we need to write the end goals that we have for ourselves and statements that we know are true because it is in God's Word. Statements such as,

"I am fearfully and wonderfully made."

"I am God's masterpiece."

"I am enough."

"I am a leader worth following."

"I am a great friend."

"I am encouraging."

"I am a loving and supportive husband/wife/son/daughter."

"I trust in God and everything He has called me to do."

"I can do anything with Christ who strengthens me."

When we constantly see the notes and the positive messages, our brain begins to alter our thoughts and turn them into reality through the process of neuroplasticity.

> *This is the process of renewing our mind. When we see them over and over, we will start to retrain our brains.*

The important thing is to write these sticky notes in the present tense. Like it has already happened.

It has been discovered that our brain cannot tell the difference between current reality and what we tell our brain about the current reality. This means that our brain will interpret what we let in and form new thoughts and steer us toward new actions.

The lesson that Brooklynn gave on that hot, summer Sunday sums up how to deal with negative thinking in four simple steps:

1. Recognize
2. Remove
3. Replace
4. Repeat

The things expressed that day really hit home with me, and I tried to capture Brooklynn's thoughts the best that I could. She speaks a lot better than I write. To view the lesson that she gave on July 24, 2022, go to Gwinnett Church's YouTube channel, and locate the lesson titled "Mindshift."

I will summarize the immense power that our thoughts have on our actions by referring to two sources (if you are a fan of Zig, then you know they go hand in hand). In the Easy-to-Read (ERV) translation of the Bible, Proverbs 4:23 reads,

"Above all, be careful what you think because your thoughts control your life."

> You are what you are, and you are where you are because of what has gone into your mind. You change what you are, and you change where you are by changing what goes into your mind.

—Zig Ziglar

» Be intentional with your thoughts and what you let in your mind.

» Remove the bad thoughts and replace them with positive thoughts.

» Repeat the process of renewing your mind. Do it over and over and over. It takes time.

FINAL THOUGHTS

I hope that you enjoyed this snapshot of some of the lessons taught by the people I have met over the years. Words cannot describe the appreciation that I have for the people mentioned in this little book and their willingness to share their stories. My heartfelt thanks go out to Thom Jacquet, Tim Baker, Barry Lindler, Tom Sikes, Phil Woody, Julie Williams, Eddie and Becky Martin, and Brooklynn Warren.

You folks are awesome!

The purpose of this book is not to beat people over the head with the Bible or to endorse organized religion. It's not. I am not a preacher or biblical scholar. I'm just a guy. A guy who is scratching the itch to be like my dad[11] and hopefully help someone who is facing an uncertain situation. I am just a guy who has met some amazing people who have seen their way through some unique challenges, and they have been willing to share their stories with me and you.

All the people mentioned, including me, have a strong belief in God and His Son, Jesus. We believe that a personal relationship with Jesus is a *must have* and that it makes life better. It won't make it easier, but it will make it immensely *better.* Our common belief is that God is for us and not against us. He will never leave us. He is our biggest cheerleader. He wants us to talk to Him, rely on Him, and love Him like He is our Father. Because He is. He is our heavenly Father.

One area that I have always been unsure about is the best way to treat someone going through a rough patch or a "bump" in life. I am not talking about the normal, daily challenges that we all face. I have always questioned how to approach someone facing a loss of some kind. Should I bring up the situation or should I ignore it and keep the conversation as normal as possible? I'm hurting along with the individual, and I want them to know that I care, but I don't want to remind them that they are going through a bad situation.

When asked about this, Julie said to just "read the room" and respond accordingly. She relayed a time when a friend approached her after Shane passed away. Her friend came up to her just devastated and sobbed throughout their entire conversation. Julie was in good spirits at the time, but her friend brought her back down and killed the mood.

People mean well. Sometimes, we don't know how to react.

Becky agreed that we should acknowledge the situation. Don't ignore the *elephant in the room*, and then the person experiencing the grief, etc., will guide you on where to go with the conversation. If they say something inappropriate (or stupid), then give them some grace and know that deep down, they are trying to help.

We cannot fix the situation almost 100% of the time. Don't try. Sometimes the best thing to say is *nothing*. Just be there and listen if the other person wants to talk.

*The gift of a listening ear and your presence is
the best way you can show your love and support
for a friend. [Julie said.]*

And, for crying out loud, do not say, "Let me know if there's anything I can do." That is a cop-out and is a way that we let ourselves off the hook. If you see something that can be done to help, do it. Don't ask. Just do it.

My life has been somewhat dull by modern-day standards. I have never had much of a redemption story or tales of overcoming and persevering. I have been happily married (to the same wife) for over twenty-nine years. My kids are wonderful, and my wife and I didn't have to wrestle with any major issues while raising them. We all enjoy spending time with each other.

Sure, my life hasn't always been easy, but it has been relatively smooth sailing compared to what others have encountered. I have never had to battle any major disease, setback, or dependency. I have never been full of despair or totally out of control. My wife, dog, and I live in a nice house surrounded by nice neighbors and friends. All in all, I have been blessed to live a blissfully boring life.

Ever since I wrote my first book (*Tight Lines & Good Selling*), I thought that it would be interesting to collect the stories and experiences of some of the people that I have "rubbed shoulders with" over the years. I have benefited from seeing them live their lives and thought that their experiences could help other people find hope, inspiration, and encouragement as they go through the twists and turns of life. If this little book can help at least one person get through a rough patch that they are going through, it is a win and worth all the time and effort of putting this together.

I have already met this goal even prior to publishing this book. The stories and experiences that are described in the preceding pages have helped *me*.

It is relatively easy to talk about personal stories from other people. It's much harder to talk about what is currently going on in my own life. While trying to wrap things up on this project—talk about timing—I am facing a "bump" of my own.

To the best of my knowledge, this "bump"—possibly a "pothole"—first came to my attention around seven years ago while we were on a family vacation at the beach. The condo where we were staying had hardwood floors and tile throughout. I was making my way to bed after everyone else had retreated to their rooms, and I remember hearing my daughter yell, "Dad, pick up your feet!" I was shuffling to the point that she could hear me through the door to her bedroom. I didn't think anything of it at the time.

Ever since then, my stride has shortened, and my balance has been slowly affected. I have experienced several slow-motion falls, but I just thought that I was being clumsy. On my walks around the neighborhood, my lower back would stiffen, and I would break out the heating pad once I got home to relieve the tightness. I would stretch and see a chiropractor on a regular basis.

My family and even a few well-meaning neighbors that would see me stumbling around the 'hood would tell me that I needed to get things checked out by a physician, but I really didn't want to. What you don't know won't hurt you, right? It was dumb on my part, but I did not want to hear that I had Parkinson's disease, ALS, or some sort of tumor. Plus, our health insurance isn't the best when it comes to out-of-pocket expenses, and we didn't/don't have a lot of extra money sitting around looking for ways to be spent.

The decision to see a physician came after being the recipient of help at my local grocery store. I was stumbling to my truck with a few bags of groceries when a nice, young man offered to help me. I truly appreciated his offer, but I realized that things were getting ridiculous. I should be the person offering help, not receiving it! This was the third time within the week that someone had noticed my situation and offered to assist. It dawned on me that I shouldn't be shuffling through life like a gimpy old man, so I decided to go to a doctor to get things checked out (like my wife and kids had been saying for a long time).

A family friend is an orthopedic surgeon, and he immediately referred me to a neurologist after he checked me out. *Oh boy.* Well, after a number of very thorough exams and X-rays, three MRIs, and nine blood tests, they can't definitively tell me what is causing my issues. It has been diagnosed as hereditary spastic paraparesis, where something is weakening my spinal cord, causing my legs, hips, and balance to be affected. The catch is that the cause is not crystal clear. The MRIs, X-rays, and blood tests all show nothing out of the ordinary. According to them, everything looks great, and I'm as healthy as anyone my age. The neurologist is confident that a hereditary gene is the cause and that there is no quick fix or cure. According to the doctor, it is what it is.

Since the neurologist could not prescribe a "fix" for my issues, and my chiropractor believes that it will be a lengthy process to lessen the lack of flexibility and balance, I decided that I would outwork it. Stretch more. Walk more. Exercise more. Eat healthier. Start swimming again.

As I am writing this, I am fifty-seven years old. If I had a say in things, I would prefer to have the mobility of other people my age and not shuffle around, stumble, and fall for the remainder of my time here on earth.

The next step in my plan to deal with this diagnosis was to join a gym that provided a place to swim/lift/exercise so I could regain my lost athleticism, so I narrowed down the list of health clubs in my area and arranged to take a tour of each facility. Recently, as I was getting out of my truck to head into the last gym, I lost my balance and had another slow-motion fall. My body went in one direction, and my right foot and leg went the other. Believe me, it wasn't graceful. Unfortunately for me, my pride wasn't the only thing that was damaged.

With my ankle and foot swollen twice their normal size, I went in for X-rays the following morning where I found out that my ankle was, indeed, broken. I was given a medical boot to wear, prescribed some pain medications, and told to avoid putting weight on it and not to drive.

But I need to drive and walk to do my job. I have always prided myself on maximizing my productivity and getting the most out of each day. Stiffly and gingerly moving around at a snail's pace is not ideal for making this happen. Is it time for a career change where I can work remotely—where standing and walking is kept at a minimum? Am I too old for a career change? I need to work to pay the bills. Like most people, I have financial responsibilities.

I also made a bad mistake and searched the term *hereditary spastic paraparesis* online. This did not provide uplifting information. Dr. Google listed multiple sources that painted not-so-rosy pictures concerning the length, treatment, and outcome of this diagnosis.

My outlook on things was not great. I was beginning to get a severe case of stinkin' thinkin'. And this is where the experiences of my friends come into play.

I remember Becky saying that "nothing good ever came from feeling sorry for myself." She had just lost a child—a major event not to be compared with my mobility and balance issues.

Eddie reminded me that *not* working is *not* an option and that God has always taken care of me and will help me through this.

Phil's story illustrates that my daily challenges are nothing compared to what others go through.

Julie told her girls (and me) that we can choose to be a victim of our circumstances or choose to overcome our circumstances and use them to make us stronger. And it helps to laugh at things along the way.

Thom spoke about preparation, confidence, gratitude, and the beneficial impact on my daily performance when I avoid the highs and lows that pop up along the way.

Tim's experiences as a soldier reminded me to "suck it up and drive on." His observation as an art teacher also hit me between the eyes as I work to finish this project—just start, and don't be afraid to make a mistake.

Tom's story is one of helping others. When I help someone else, it makes me forget about my own issues, and it floods me with gratitude and appreciation.

Barry reminded me that staying positive isn't always easy and takes a good deal of effort, but having a positive mindset greatly impacts how I feel and act and how others interact with me. If he remained positive through his "bumps," then I should be able to think and feel positive through my "bumps."

Piggybacking on Barry's story was the lesson that Brooklynn presented. She gave me a blueprint on how to retrain my mind so that I remove and destroy my negative thoughts and replace them with positive thoughts.

As I close this book, I will read it over and over to express things in the best way and to find anything that could be better written. You know, proofread it. I am more concerned in finding grammatical errors than I am *listening* to the words and stories. After my recent medical findings and escapades, I finally *heard* the advice that my friends gave.

It helps.

The individuals mentioned in the previous stories all faced uncertain and challenging situations. Through their stories, they pointed us to a smoother path where the "bumps" and "potholes" aren't as jarring.

It takes a tremendous amount of effort on our part to internally compete and be intentional about maintaining a positive mindset and combine the positive outlook with a rock-solid reliance on our faith. It isn't easy. It's a grind. It's exhausting. But—as my friends showed us—*it can be done.*

We learn from the experiences of others. And we *can* turn the "bumps" and "potholes" into amazing opportunities for growth.

Like I stated earlier, if this little book encourages and assists at least one person in finding their way through the "bumps" or "potholes" they are facing, I've met my goal. I can claim victory, do the happy dance (even though I can't dance), and feel that I am a small part of the solution.

Well, I won. It *is* helping me. And I hope it helps you.

~*~

If we are observant, we will find inspiring stories all around us. These examples on how to deal with the "bumps" in life don't necessarily come from highly visible people. We can find incredible examples from our friends, parents, co-workers, neighbors, and every other unsuspecting source. We just need to be open to seeing them.

Thank you for taking the time to read this.

Author Jon Wright invites you to visit and connect with him at www.JonWright.us.

ENDNOTES

[1] The second-highest rank a non-commissioned officer can achieve behind only the Sergeant Major of the Army who reports directly to the Chief of Staff. A CSM is the most senior member of a color-bearing Army unit, such as a battalion.

[2] Sikes Media: sikesmedia.com, facebook.com/SikesMedia/, twitter.com/MediaSikes

[3] Prospect Presbyterian Church: prospectpc.org, facebook.com/ProspectPC

[4] Missionscape, missionscape.com; facebook.com/PavingYourWay; Walking for Kids Foundation, walkingforkids.org; Presbytery of Mississippi, pby-of-ms.com; Meridian Community College, merediancc.edu; Meridian Little Theater, meridianlittletheater.com

[5] Special Place for Others to Thrive: thespotfamily.com, facebook.com/FamilyResourceForKids

[6] Christians believe that the Holy Spirit is the third Person of the Trinity (the Father, the Son, and the Holy Spirit), and that God is spiritually active in the world through the Holy Spirit.

[7] Knox Martin Foundation for Brain Cancer Research: knoxmartinfoundation.org, facebook.com/KnoxMartinFoundation, instagram.com/KnoxMartin_Foundation

[8] Zig Ziglar was an author, salesman/sales trainer, and motivational speaker who positively influenced millions of people over his forty-plus-year career.

[9] *Psychology Today*, 2022. From press release from Queen's University dated July 13, 2020. Queensu.ca/gazette/media

[10] Gwinnett Church: gwinnettchurch.org, instagram.com/GwinnettChurch, facebook.com/GwinnettChurch, twitter.com/GwinnettChurch

[11] Paul H. Wright, Phd., was a professor of civil engineering at the Georgia Institute of Technology for over thirty-two years. He authored several textbooks focusing on civil engineering, including transportation engineering, highway engineering, and airport design and engineering.